HAMSTER

Samantha Nugent
and Jared Siemens

AV2
www.av2books.com

Step 1
Go to **www.av2books.com**

Step 2
Enter this unique code

FZIGO1LVD

Step 3
Explore your interactive eBook!

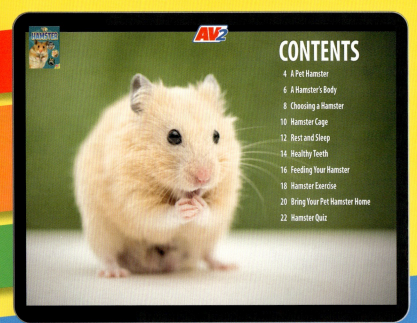

AV2

CONTENTS

AV2 is optimized for use on any device

Your interactive eBook comes with...

Contents
Browse a live contents page to easily navigate through resources

Audio
Listen to sections of the book read aloud

Videos
Watch informative video clips

Weblinks
Gain additional information for research

Try This!
Complete activities and hands-on experiments

Key Words
Study vocabulary, and complete a matching word activity

Quizzes
Test your knowledge

Slideshows
View images and captions

This title is part of our AV2 digital subscription

1-Year Grades K–5 Subscription ISBN
978-1-7911-3320-7

Access hundreds of AV2 titles with our digital subscription.
Sign up for a FREE trial at **www.av2books.com/trial**

2

HAMSTER

CONTENTS

A Pet Hamster

Hamsters are originally from Asia. They were first discovered in the deserts of Syria, where they made deep **burrows** in the sand. Hamsters were first brought to the United States in 1938. By 2004, one out of every three U.S. households had a pet hamster.

Today, hamsters are the most popular small pets in the world. Hamsters require regular care and attention, and should be taken to a veterinarian if they exhibit any **abnormal** behavior.

 Hamsters are **small and soft**. They are also relatively simple to care for.

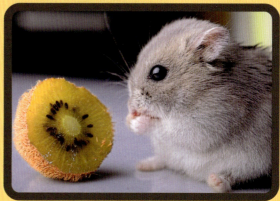

Hamster Burrow

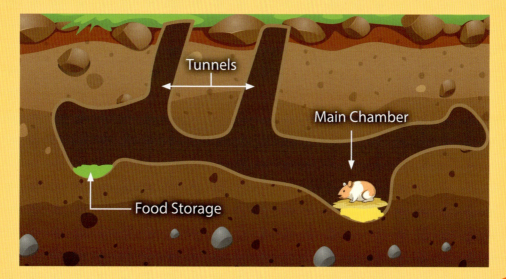

Tunnels

Main Chamber

Food Storage

Nose

Hamsters have a very strong sense of smell. They use their noses to identify food and other hamsters.

A Hamster's Body

Hamsters belong to a large group of animals called **rodents**. Each **breed** of hamster has unique characteristics, but all hamsters have certain features in common.

Ears
Hamsters have very strong hearing. With their thin, delicate ears, they can hear sounds that people cannot.

Eyes
Hamsters have large, bulging eyes. However, they do not see very well in daylight or at close range.

Paws
Hamsters use their paws for many things, including grooming, digging, holding food, and emptying their cheek pouches.

Choosing a Hamster

Hamsters range in size from 2 to 13.4 inches (5 to 34 centimeters). Pet hamsters generally have short tails and **stocky** bodies. A hamster's feet can be furry or hairless, depending on its breed.

There are five types of hamsters that people keep as pets. Syrian hamsters are the most commonly kept hamster **species**.

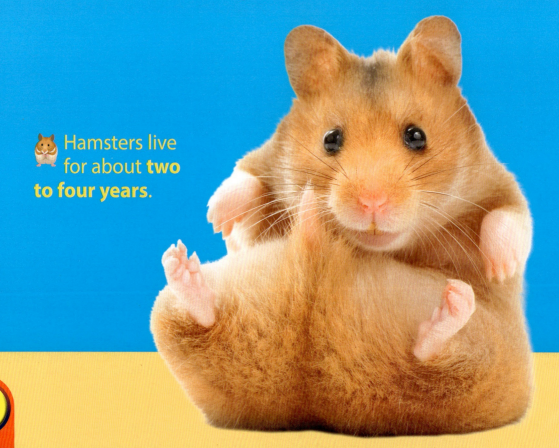

Hamsters live for about **two to four years**.

Five Main Hamster Species

2–3 inches
Roborovski Hamster

3–4 inches
Winter White Dwarf Hamster

4 inches
Chinese Hamster

4 inches
Campbell's Dwarf Hamster

5–7 inches
Syrian Hamster

Hamster Cage

Hamsters are often kept in wire cages with plastic bottoms. The cages may be lined with timothy hay or wood shavings. Tubes and tunnels can be placed in a cage to let the hamster explore and exercise. Some hamster species must live alone, while others prefer a companion.

Hamster cages need to be cleaned every week. This includes removing and replacing any soiled bedding. Uneaten food should be removed daily from the cage before it spoils.

A hamster cage **should have a wheel** for your hamster to run in.

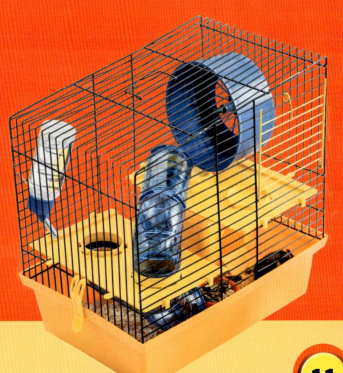

Rest and Sleep

Pet hamsters like to hide and sleep in enclosed places, such as small boxes or flowerpots. Hamsters are nocturnal. This means they sleep during the day and are active at night.

Placing your hamster's cage in a quiet place will allow your hamster to rest during the day. Hamsters can develop stress-related illnesses if their cages are kept near noisy places.

Hamster Fact

Hamsters sleep **all day long**.

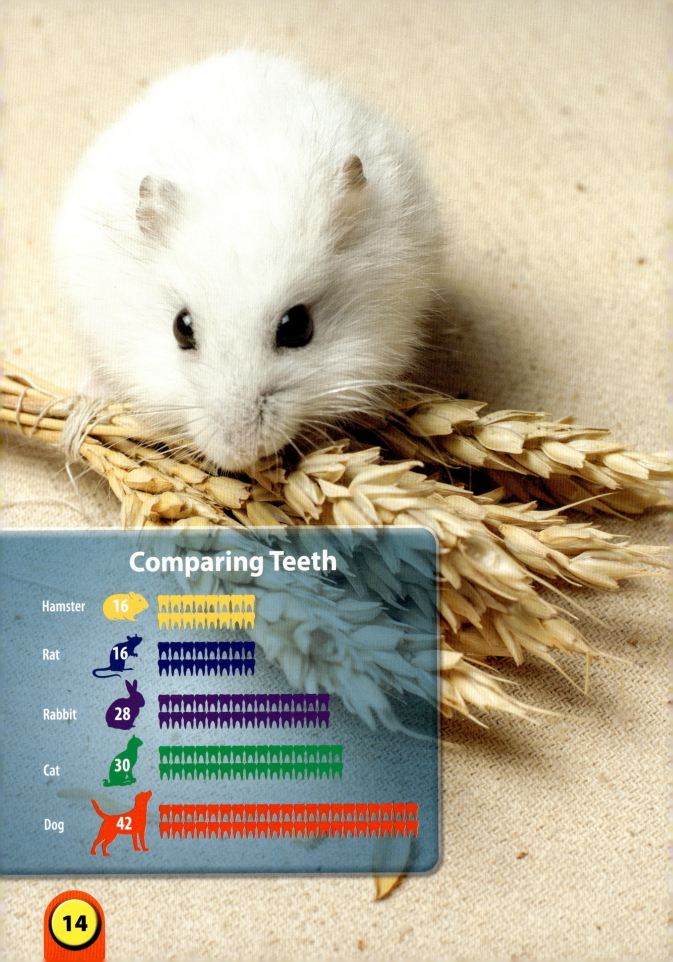

Comparing Teeth

Hamster	16	
Rat	16	
Rabbit	28	
Cat	30	
Dog	42	

Healthy Teeth

The long upper and lower teeth at the front of a hamster's mouth are called **incisors**. As these teeth never stop growing, they must be worn down by chewing.

Hamster owners often give their pets pieces of clean wood to chew. Plastic toys should not be given to hamsters to **gnaw** on, as they may pose a choking **hazard**.

Hamsters have a **total of 16 teeth**, including 4 incisors and 12 molars.

Feeding Your Hamster

Hamsters should be fed once daily, usually in the evening or night when they are most active. A hamster needs a balanced diet, including a mix of seeds, grains, cracked corn, and pellets. This can be **supplemented** with fresh fruits and vegetables every few days.

Hamsters need a specially designed water bottle. The bottle should be filled with fresh water each day.

Hamster Fact

Hamsters **stuff their cheeks** with food to eat later.

Hamster Exercise

Hamsters can safely play outside of their cages in plastic hamster balls or play pens. Owners should **supervise** their hamster when it is out of its cage to make sure it does not escape or encounter dangers, such as other pets.

Hamsters also enjoy tunneling through cardboard tubes for entertainment and exercise.

Hamster Fact

A hamster can run up to **8 miles** (13 kilometers) each day.

Bring Your Pet Hamster Home

Hamsters may need more time to bond with humans than other small pets do. New hamster owners will need to be patient as their hamster **adjusts** to its new home. Once the hamster is used to the smell of its owner, the owner may try to gently pick it up.

A hamster should always be held near the ground in case of accidental falls. Hamsters may become sick if they are handled too much.

 Hamsters **use their whiskers** to help feel their way around.

HAMSTER QUIZ

1 Where are hamsters originally from?

2 How long do hamsters live?

3 What are the long upper and lower teeth at the front of a hamster's mouth called?

4 When were hamsters first brought to the United States?

5 Are a hamster's feet furry or hairless?

6 How many miles can a hamster run each day?

Answers

1. Asia 2. About two to four years 3. Incisors 4. In 1938 5. It depends on the breed 6. Up to 8 miles (13 km)

KEY WORDS

abnormal: unusual

adjusts: becomes used to

breed: a group of animals that share specific characteristics

burrows: holes or tunnels dug by small animals for shelter

gnaw: bite at or chew on something persistently

hazard: danger

incisors: sharp teeth at the front of the mouth that are used for cutting

rodents: mammals with teeth designed for nibbling or gnawing

species: a group of similar animals that can reproduce with each other

stocky: broad, short, and solidly built

supervise: keep watch over

supplemented: added to something in order to improve it

INDEX

Get the best of both worlds.

AV2 bridges the gap between print and digital.

The expandable resources toolbar enables quick access to content including **videos**, **audio**, **activities**, **weblinks**, **slideshows**, **quizzes**, and **key words**.

Animated videos make static images come alive.

Resource icons on each page help readers to further **explore key concepts**.

Published by AV2
276 5th Avenue
Suite 704 #917
New York, NY 10001
Website: www.av2books.com

Library of Congress Cataloging-in-Publication Data

Names: Nugent, Samantha, author. | Siemens, Jared, author.
Title: Hamster / Samantha Nugent and Jared Siemens.
Description: New York, NY : AV2, [2022] | Series: My favorite pet |
   Includes index. | Audience: Ages 8-11 | Audience: Grades 2-3
Identifiers: LCCN 2020053919 (print) | LCCN 2020053920 (ebook) | ISBN
   9781791135096 (library binding) | ISBN 9781791135102 (paperback) | ISBN
   9781791135119
Subjects: LCSH: Hamsters as pets--Juvenile literature.
Classification: LCC SF459.H3 N84 2022 (print) | LCC SF459.H3 (ebook) |
   DDC 636.935/6--dc23
LC record available at https://lccn.loc.gov/2020053919
LC ebook record available at https://lccn.loc.gov/2020053920

Printed in Guangzhou, China
1 2 3 4 5 6 7 8 9 0 25 24 23 22 21

012021
101120

Project Coordinator: Priyanka Das
Designer: Terry Paulhus